WHAT IF WE REWRITE "THE STARS"

IT WAS OVER BUT SOMEHOW MY BROKEN HEART STILL FOUND ITS WAY TO BEAT.

SRISHTI SINGH

Made with ❤ on the Notion Press Platform
www.notionpress.com

To my masi,

Kanchan Singh

who always supported and motivated me in this journey.

Masi,

I hope wherever you are right now, you'd be proud of me...

Contents

Contents

Foreword

"We all are poets,
in our own way.
The only difference is that -
Some write poetries

Some become the reason of those poetries.....!!!"

1. IMAGINATION

On a starry night,
Under the starry sky
The night wind blew,
You looked in my eyes
Holding my hands
you placed your lips on mine
Millions of feelings
rushed through my mind.
The feelings that words couldn't define
or
Maybe it was just an
imagination of mine......

2. YOU ARE BEAUTIFUL

The beauty that is unseen at times,
The pretty faces, burnt in acid alkalines.
The thousands of surgeries performed on faces in lines,
The people out there blaming the feminine for her happenings in life.
For whom shall she trust on people out there,
Where her own people left her on mid-way to cry.
The purity of heart that is rejected for public showtime,
For the selfish people just care for their high price.
Who shall make her understand,
That she can redefine beauty in her own way,
For she needs to know this fact for her lifetime joy!!!

3. TOGETHER FOREVER

Walking towards an unknown path,
Where all the doors are closed for both the hearts.
People curse them for holding each others hand,
But they still continue to walk from the people apart.
They've reached a point in life,
Where they need nothing,
But each others faith.
They promise to stay together for their lifetime,
And have become each others breath.
Their life without each other,
Will reach to no place but death.
The presence of each other makes them strong,
A hope to stay along for lifelong!!!

4. SHADES OF INVISIBLE

The sun shone brighter that day,
I thought I'll have something tremendous on my way.
The skies looked charmer and gay,
I hoped that I'll acquire something special on my tray.
The surrounding looked cheerful, I can say,
For I came to know that now I'm ready to enjoy.
After days of months I see an endearing smile on my face.
The heart and mind both mumble,
They see a shining light ray.
For I wished for nothing so big by the way,
But to get a bit more crazy to slay.
I just needed my people to make me happy,
That's all I can crave for myself to stay.
But the moments passed and passed by,
I didn't find any reason to dance ballet and play with my clay.
The clouds started gathering suddenly,
The thunder and lightning started knocking at my gateway,
The tress with full vivacity began to sway.
My heartbeat fastened untimely,
My mind went all blank and empty.
It was the sign of a terror deadly day.
Everything changed in a second,
And took me at a point to cry high.
The reason behind it,

I would not like to now replay,
My beloved ones are now moved away.
My heart has now became stony,
My face is all dried and ugly.
That one incident changed my life,
Brought me at a stage where everything is BETRAYED!!!!

5. THE LAST LETTER

Slowly,
I'll take a walk to the heaven
Sit there, and watch you every single day.
I'll be happy being there
watching you,
And send you the signals
Letting you know
I never went away. I'll listen to your endless chatterings
Reply them back
Which you'll hear through your heartstrings
But yell inside for me to comeback.
Remembering our flashbacks
Maybe those tears will fall
Which will take away your sleeps
But-
I'll still be there
Holding you while you weep.
Inside you'll be only wishing for one thing
A wish-begging to have me home. I'll try to send you signs
So that you know— you are not alone.
Don't feel lonely
Just don't live in agony that you have "life" —
that was taken away from me.
Heaven is a beautiful sight

You'll have to see it some day at the right time.
Till then-
Just hold on for a while
Live your life
Laugh for every single time
Be free
Then I know-
With every breath you take
You'll be taking one for me!!!

6. SISTER

Crying on a rainy night,
Waiting for someone special to fall at my sight.
Feeling the droplets of water falling to my right.
Suddenly I hear the sound of my heart,
Whispering me to smile bright,
For someone special has arrived to light up my life.
The one who will bring all of us a lot of pride.
That one asks for nothing,
but a little love for her hope giving smile.
Seeing her reminds me of birds taking long flights.
She wishes for nothing,
But people to stand by her side.
That one beautiful person arrived in my life,
Like a sudden shine in a dark night.
I gave up my heart to her in a while,
For I know she will keep it alright.
Love to eternity is all what I want to give her,
For I know she will be my best sister at my good and bad times!!!

7. BEHIND MY SHADOW

I tried to create my own fantasy,
But I stepped back.
I tried to build up my own dreams,
But fear of nonfeasance attacked.
I tried looking up to those shining stars,
Thinking where I lacked.
I tried dancing up to my own music,
To get a bit relaxed.
I tried cheering up to my own glasses,
Getting a feeling of living in a world of black.
I tried to sing myself on my birthday,
To avoid my emptiness fact.
I tried stimulating myself at times,
But couldn't forget those nightmare flashbacks.
I tried, tried and tried.....
But could never thrive my daydream tracks.
I see a gloomy vision of myself walking around,
Trying to knock back.
People telling to listen up my brain,
Shadows telling to listen up my heart,
Questions bouncing in my head front and back.
I get afraid seeing those apparition at times,
But although now I can't overcome this bitter FACT!!!

8. I'M STRONG

Take me to an outside world,
Where my past can be hurled.
Take me to a place,
Where I can have my own space.
Take me somewhere so apart,
Where I can again restart.
Thousands of dreams are still left to be fulfilled,
And I again want to be refilled.
The steps to be walked maybe too long,
But still I can walk along,
For I am still not shattered,
For I am still too strong after being frowned!!!!

9. WHEN WE MET

When we met,
My motive of life changed.
I never felt that love can be this alluring.
We saw a shining elation in each other's eye,
A different world where we can survive.
You kept my dreams fulfilling,
Just to make me smile.
You tried to control my anger with stupid jokes which weren't even funny sometimes.
Still it was always a beautiful try,
For it always made my heart filled with butterflies.
A single drop of tear from my eye,
Made your heart to cry for a longtime.
You are someone much more my soul could have ever asked for.
Now let's hold each other's hand,
and take a walk though sunshine.
Let's create a heavenly destiny where we will live for our lifetime!!!

10. NATURAL MAGIC

The clouds gather,
The darkness larger.
The sunshine disappears,
The light unclear.
The trees dance,
The grasses enhance.
The ocean waves move,
The beaches land cools.
The buds that grow,
The flowers that glow.
The dolphins that swim,
The birds that scream.
The rain that falls,
The nature when calls.
The earth that shines,
The creatures when smile!!!!

11. FOREVER AND ALWAYS

'LOVE' was a simple word,
Just a normal word with four letters,
Far away from my imaginations,
Where I never wished to get emerged.
In the turning of twilight,
And the shadows of moonlight,
I found someone like you.
Who's eyes danced with mine,
And stole my sleeps at night.
You have sparkles of stars
in your eyelid,
And a universe within your soul,
That bewitched me to
your ceaseless heart,
Like a pull of a black hole.
You are my wish
I craft on those shooting stars,
A whole galaxy
Where I would slumber
And you will be near holding me
In your soothing arms.
Under the sheets of the sky

Our legs intertwined,
As I tenderly paint
The hue of my lips along yours.
Caress your back,
Runinng my fingers through your hairs,
Losing all my tracks.
And how when we will stare
At each other?
Only both of us will be there,
Everything around will disappear.
And there are so many things
I would plan out to do,
I have wanted for so long
The waits I know would never get over.
But I really don't wish to get out of this reverie,
Even if I have to wait for thousand more "ETERNITIES"!!!

12. WHY NOT WHY?

On a cloudy morning,
Waking up with so many
New thoughts in mind.
Looking in the mirror,
With hundreds of expectations to thrive.
New dreams to be fulfilled,
New challenges to be challenged,
New world to be created,
New, new and new.....
But what happens in a while?
The expectations are broken,
Dreams get rotten,
Challenges are losen,
Creating new world gets forgotten,
The whole day comes to an end,
The night enters,
The twenty-four hours seems to be wasted.
Screaming starts,
Tears start rollin' down the eyes,
Crying begins.
But is this fine? Is it okay?
Why not fighting things back?
Why not sorting things out?
Why not why?

Always remains a question in reality.
Creating new fantasies,
Fulfilling thousand of dreams,
Completing all the challenges,
Always remains a VIRTUALITY!!!!

13. YOU & I

I had everything in life,
But still waited for something bright.
I never knew what this relation was of you and I,
But now I have answers for every questions in my mind.
For now I have you by my side,
And together we have to walk a thousand distant miles.
I know you are not giving upon me anytime,
For I am your forever love in your life.
Together we have made hundreds of memories,
But that's still too short for our endless love life.
The memories spent with you are my favourite moments.
Remembering them brings me a lot of smile.
Our first tight hug made me so much delight after that long cry.
Our first soft kiss made me feel so special after that unexpected fight.
The way we play with our hanky,
That shows a cute couple sign.
Though we still have many moments left to rewind
And many to fall in upcoming times.
For I know I will always have you at my sight.
What else do I need now,
My life is already complete as you have entered to make it shine.
Now don't go away from me,
For you stole my heart and took my hands,
And now you have to keep it alright.

You and I we are two love birds who are meant to fly,
Together we are one soul who will keep on shining forever bright!!!

14. BROTHER

Somehow, Somewhere
Everyone's heart got its way to beat,
Somehow, Somewhere I got a baby brother to play with.
Scattering light through his elysian smile,
Keeps our life bright.
Someone who's one divine laugh,
Warms up my heart.
Someone who's one shriek of cry,
Tears up my soul apart.
Someone who's lofty nature,
Cheers up our day to start.
Someone who's his mother's hope of light,
Someone who's her dream of night.
Someone who's his father's silver lining,
Someone who's the reason he is alive.
Someone who is the charm of everyone's life,
Someone who will represent all of us at great heights,
Someone who's just everything that will help us survive.
This new happiness kept us delight.
But evil's eye splashed on everyone's life.
Silence began to roam all around,
Darkness escalated on hills and ground.
The moment of happiness turned into family people's crying sound.
Society victimizes, cares for nothing.

Everyone gets broken and feels drowned,
Suffering to calibrate the boy,
So that he's again safe and sound.
Evil's eye splashes in everyone's life,
But this can't ravage our sunshine.
Can't let a single drop of water fall from my eye,
For I know god is by our side.
Why to cry we just have to try,
For I know there's a heavenly morning after a pernicious night.

15. LOVE

"Love can forever be your beautiful escape---

Or

It can forever be your lifelong mistake"

16. DON'T FORGET TO FLY

Life isn't a duck soup,
This world isn't that comely,
If you want to precept here----
You need to get out from your own bounds of possibility,
Only then you'll be a crowned head of your DESTINY!!!

17. HOW LONG?

Life wasn't this idyllic before,
Was it just because—
you weren't here
to help me explore?
Is this
a real love?
Or just
a proximity?
Will this last
for eternity?
Or you'll
snuff me out
ETERNALLY?

18. PRETTY WOMAN

You are such
beauty—
inside & outside.
The rainbow
shines,
through your
appealing eyes.
The gold,
is right–right
underneath your chest,
a golden heart
that is
so pure & precious.
Your eyes—
the diamonds,
that illuminates
and
fave that brightens up
someone's day to
'STAY'!!!

19. BETTER TOGETHER

I desire to—
evade myself
in your
enamoured arms,
Lay out my soul
to yours.
Forget that
I've a name
Live for
each other's entity.
And become the kind of
elegant that is
only found
in our
Hearts!!

20. TEARS IN HEAVEN

Everyday,
I endeavor—
endeavor to detach
the agony
of our separation
concealed in
my broken heart!!!

21. SENSE OF LOVE

Love is a tale that is forever left undefined.

22. I KNOW

Trust me,
I know—
I know exactly how it feels to—
find moments
where you can drop your fake smile,
where you can cry,
cry when there is nobody hearing,
when there is nobody looking.
I know—
I know exactly how it feels to—
stand in front of the mirror,
staring yourself
with tears in your eyes,
questioning your own entity.
I know—
I know exactly how it feels—
When you try—
try to mend all those pain scars,
you disguised in your soul
so far.
I know—
I know exactly how it feels to—
lock the door knob
and

scream so hard.
I know—
I know exactly how it feels to—
bury your happiness
in your ruptured heart.
I know—
I know exactly how it feels—
when you're done—
done with each and every single thing,
and you fall apart.
A point where you wish
everything to end,
where you don't want to restart.
I know—
I know exactly how—
tough it is
to be once again
healed.
I know—
I know exactly how it feels—
to feel this way!!!

23. DRUNK

I am—

'drunk in our love.'

The "drinks"—

I don't ever want to get rid off!!!

24. YOU REALIZE

For someday,
Suddenly when you are done
with every single situation
happening in your life.
You realize-
You are not okay!
That at night
When the world falls asleep
chasing their dreams.
You stay awake
Fighting with the demons
inside your entire being.
You realize,
You have no one by your side,
No one to see
even if you are alright.
You realize,
You wanted to talk about it,
You wanted to scream, yell
and shout about it.
But all you could do was
keep yourself quiet
and
whisper you are just fine.

You realize,
That those old wound scars disguised,
never genuinely heals
and bleed again and again
at the slightest word
with passing time.
You realize
Your heart is tangled,
Your brain is a chaos,
and
Now you can't have
one more fight.
And when the first drop of tear
falls from your eyes,
That's when you realize,
You have lost
all your forbearance
and have lost all those reasons
to stay alive.
And that's how
You end up your
"LIFE"!!!

25. HOLD MY HAND

Hold my hand,
My love—
We'll fly—
fly to the sky
far away from this sight.
Where there will be noone
to make us cry.
Where we'll always
grin with delight
around the stars
twinkling bright.
With an appealing glamour
in our eyes,
we'll fly with no sigh,
like two heavenly kites
with ignite in their flight,
we'll fly with full excite,
to be each other's strength
till we die.
Hold my hand,
My love—
We'll fly—
fly high to the sky,
to a site full of divine light,

a site meant for only
You & I!!!

26. TRAPPED

Sometimes,
I feel too much at once.
Other times,
I feel nothing at all.
I really don't know what's worse:
Suffocating within the air
or
Suffocating without it!!!

27. TAINTED LOVE

It's been years
since we were pulled apart.
Still I've—
Treasured our moments
safely in my heart.
I don't really know why—
why I can't leave you behind.
Even though I know—
I know—
These agonies, these tears—
they all are
just because of you.
I want to hate you,
to start a life anew,
to accomplish all those dreams
I had wanted to pursue.
To live a life
without you.
But for every moment,
When I try doing this,
I come to know—
"I'm falling for you even more"

28. MIDNIGHT MOONLIGHT

Back
to the moon....
Perhaps,
it was the only one
with whom—
I used to
spend my nights
before
I met you!
Perhaps,
now it is the only one
with whom—
I can
spend my nights
when you are
GONE!!!

29. STARS ONLY KNOW

I love having
long conversations
with the
'STARS'!
They tell me
about the
'MOON'—
their only love
from such
long
'ETERNITIES '!
&
I tell them
about
'YOU'—
my only love
forever till the
'END'!!!!

30. EUPHORIA

Love her to the rhythm of your
'HEART'
&
You'll feel ecstasy like never before!!!

31. IMPERFECTLY PERFECT

"She was his life
And he was her all
They loved each other
And they were happy together"
A perfect love story, isn't it?
But can all love stories
be the perfect one like this?
Loving is not always blissful,
even a beautiful rose can have dark shades
That we are apart from each other
Doesn't mean our love will fade.
You became my sunshine
When I only saw the rain
You gave me happiness
When I only felt the pain
Then why do I feel lonely again?
You and I are like summer and winter
We endlessly chase each other.
But one has to leave
for the other to come,
Cause we cannot be together .
I'll love you forever with all my heart

My love for you will never end
Maybe our story is not perfect
That's why this story is different
Not every love story needs to be perfect
But for that love will not be less
Not all words need to be expressed
Cause our story is 'imperfectly perfect"!!!

32. DIAMOND

You are a diamond—
You shine through the darkness
and
Stand strong like a stone.
You are a diamond—
You fight like a warrior
Inspite
all the immortal wickedness
through which you have
gone!!!

33. SCARS

Your scars—
are not something,
you have to be ashamed of.
Each one of them—
is an angelic line,
combining to make a
"POETRY"
of fascinating pattern
of rhymes,
telling a beautiful story.
And
Love it because—
Not only you,
But
The whole world loves
"POETRY"
and the story hidden
behind it!!!

34. BEHIND ME

There's a girl behind me—
Friendly with many,
Enjoys with nobody.
Laughs with any.
Do you even know?
Inside she is buried!
There's a girl behind me—
Locks her face within her palms,
Whispers she is feeling calm.
In reality,
She locks that she is harmed,
And cry all night,
Losing all her charm!
There's a girl behind me—
Says she doesn't care.
The world says—
"She is scared."
She shows she is fine.
Inside she is broken to bits and pieces
for such a long time.
Who knows?
Inside she is just a dead body
who lost her life!!!

35. WHY POETRIES?

They asked-
"Why do you love poetries ?"
I answered-
"Because unlike other people
they were never
afraid to touch me,
when I was all bruised and broken!!!"

36. I'LL BE BACK HOME

If I ever lose my mind,
Embrace me tight
&
I promise-
For eternity-
I'll be there back home-
Back to my life-
"YOU"

37. JUST A WARM HUG

Sometimes,
All I want is-
You to
Enclose me
when I-
screech so high.
Because I'm
tired of the
affliction called
'THOUGHT'
lingering in my
mind!!!

38. DROWNING

Each and every
Single day-
I'm drowning-
Drowning in the ocean-
Of our
"MEMORIES"

39. YOU'RE MY FAVOURITE

The sweet melody of your voice---
is my favourite song that keeps playing in my ears
all the time.
The soft finger of yours when intertwines my skin---
is my favourite moment that keeps rewinding in my
mind.
The warm and safe place where you reside me in
your heart---
is my favourite place where my soul always wishes
to hide.
The fragrance of your body when embraces mine---
is my favourite smell I have liked.
is my favourite flavour I always want to bite.
The taste of your cherry lips---
The glamour of your eyes when stares mine---
is my favourite view that pleasure my eyes.
Amongst all the creations--- you are my favourite one and Forever you are
"mine"!!!

40. CHERRY LIPS

Our lips
Run wild,
On each others
"SKIN"
And
This is
"SERENITY"
What I feel!!!

41. MIDNIGHT WONDERS

When the night falls
I stare through my window
Look at those stars
And watch them glow
Among those twinkling stars
When the moon shines bright
I wonder if you were here by my side
Holding hands, we could spend this night
I wonder about the dream
That I always cherish in my heart
I wonder if this dream breaks
Will I be able to fix those broken parts ?
When the night falls deep,
I close my eyes but can't sleep
I just embrace the silence of the night
I feel like you are here by my side
Telling me that everything will be alright
I wonder if it's a dream again
Everytime I hope it isn't
I wish I could stop the time
And hold you forever
But when I open my eyes

I realize that you weren't here
Under this moon and these stars
I'm the only one here
wondering in the
Midnight!!!

42. ONCE A REALITY

You were

once the

"REALITY".

Now an

"IMAGINATION"-

I'll be

imagining

Too much!!!

43. POISON

"YOU"-
You are the
poison,
I'm addicted to.
Even though-
I know-
you're destroying me,
"BIT BY BIT"!!!

44. EVERYTHING CHANGED

My Love,
Time gradually changes-
"everything and everyone."
Even "YOU" AND "YOUR LOVE"
changed with time.

45. CAN'T REPLACE

You read-
Poetries in my mind
I could never forget.
You wrote-
Stories in my heart
I could never erase!!!

46. GOODBYE

You never said-
You'll be leaving this way.
You never said-
We'll be having a goodbye.
The bitter thought,
still lingers from the day
I tried to make you stay.
Now,
This emptiness is endless which I can't push away.
It was fine if you no more wanted
anything to say.
I was there to become your voice in
those silent days.
Now everyday,
Those stats don't seem to sparkle
in my sky,
The moon seems to fade away.
What will I crave for now? What will I do to stay?
All these million times I have needed you
A million times I have died,
If love alone could have stopped you
I never would have cried.
In life-
I love you with all of me

In dreams-
I love you still.
In my heart there is an emptiness
That only you can fill.
I miss you always.
I try searching for the answer Why did you leave me to cry?
You were gone before we knew it
And now only God knows why!!!

Acknowledgements

I feel so contended and gleeful that my first ever book is finally published. Its very obvious that this dream wouldn't have come true without the support of the precious ones of my life.

Firstly, I'd like to thank my parents Mr. Prabhat Kumar Singh and Mrs. Ranjana Singh who constantly supported me throughout this writing journey. Especially my father, who always motivated me and never left a single stone unturned for me. Thank you both of you for believing in me and showing me the bright path for my future.

To my brother, Utkarsh Raj whom I‘m eternally grateful to. Thank you for supporting me since day one and making me believe that I will surely accomplish my dream one day.

To my bestfriends, my forever ride or die- Supriya, Akshar and Nishant, without whom my journey would always be incomplete. Thank you for always being there with me whenever darkness loomed over. I truly appreciate all of your presence in my life. I love you all to bits and pieces.

To my family, My mama, mami, masis and buas, who supported me through thick and thin and helped me in each and every phase of life.

To my cousins, to whom I'm eternally grateful to. Thank you for supporting and giving me hope at times whenever I felt low.

To my writing partners- Aashi, Shiksha Di and Sushrut for always correcting me with my write-ups. Without you all I'd have never been able to correct my flaws and get better in this.

I'd like to thank to thank some of my people especially Rishika, Vaishnavi, Indira, Aditya Ratna and Harsh Giri for their constant love and support.

I would like to thank Notion press publishing team who helped me reach out to a larger audience.

Last but not the least- to my readers. Thank you to all those who picked up my book and read it. Thank you so very much. Without you all this would have been impossible.

SRISHTI SINGH

Printed by Libri Plureos GmbH in Hamburg, Germany